Lead Me to the Rock

*The Spiritual Struggle of an
Introvert in an Extroverted Church Culture*

Michael Burns
with J. Brian Craig and Reggie Hearn

Lead Me to the Rock
The Spiritual Struggle of an Introvert in an Extroverted Church

About the authors: Michael Burns (DMin Bethel University; MA Wesley Seminary, Indiana Wesleyan University) is the Congregational Teacher for the DFW Church in Dallas-Fort Worth, Texas. He is the cohost of the *Eikon Podcast*. His other books include *Crossing the Line: Culture, Race, and Kingdom; All Things to All People: The Power of Cultural Humility;*

Escaping the Beast: Politics, Allegiance, and Kingdom and *Life Is Spiritual.* He and his wife, MyCresha, have two adult children. All of Michael's books are available for purchase at www.ipibooks.com.

J. Brian Craig served for many years as both an evangelist and teacher for the South Bay Church in Los Angeles, CA. He was a talented musician and songwriter. He wrote many beloved hymns and songs, including "Praises Heard Around the World," "Anchor for the Soul," and "Be With Me, Lord." Brian passed away in 2024, survived by his wife Dessa and their three children.

Reggie Hearn has been a disciple of Jesus since 2014. He played professional basketball with several teams, including the Reno Bighorns and the Detroit Pistons. He also played for Team USA and was named the 2018 USA Basketball Male Athlete of the Year. He currently serves as a scout for the San Antonio Spurs. Reggie, his wife Gianna, and their daughter live in Las Vegas, NV.

ILLUMINATION
www.ipibooks.com   PUBLISHERS

Contents

Foreword

I became familiar with the writings of Michael Burns a few years ago, having personally interacted with him only briefly a few times before that. His work has had a significant role in helping our fellowship understand the racial, cultural, and political factors that Satan can use to assault our unity. In *Lead Me to the Rock* he insightfully addresses another serious threat, particularly damaging because it is somewhat more subtle. What is it like to be an introvert in the dominant extroverted culture of the church?

Michael writes clearly, with vulnerability but without resentment or unfair judgment, about the challenges of being an introverted person in a fellowship that has often overvalued the larger-than-life, overtly outgoing personality. His appeal to a deeper appreciation of Paul's commentary in 1 Corinthians 12 about the importance of each part and the variety of parts, comparing the church to a physical body, is timely and indicates a growing maturity in our understanding of God's design for his people.

As a predominately extroverted person, I was challenged by this book to think more deeply about the effect of our culture on the introverted among us. Ironically, I have been married for many decades to an introvert. I have seen her struggle sometimes with our church culture's expectations, particularly expectations for those in the full-time ministry. She deeply loves God and people, and God has worked through her in amazing ways. However, I witnessed her extremely effective ways of helping people being questioned sometimes by those whose personalities were different, especially in the early years of our ministry life.

I deeply appreciate Michael's inclusion of conversations with our son Brian. Many readers of this book will know of Brian and his influence in the body of Christ, especially through his music. They will probably also know that at age fifty-three he lost his two-year battle with glioblastoma brain cancer but won the victory of a faithful life.

Brian is my hero for very many reasons. He did not let being an introvert stop him from allowing God to use him, even though as he grew up, he was not the typical outgoing overachiever valued by the culture of our fellowship, especially at that time in history. He did not let potentially discouraging messages, and even specific disparaging conversations, deter him from whatever he believed to be God's plan for his life. Consequently, he left a great legacy of a life surrendered to God and used by God.

I appreciate Michael's appeal to introverts to relish how God has made them and the strengths they have. I am challenged, especially as an elder, to help those of us who are more extroverted realize the implications we often convey and the atmosphere we create.

Michael recognized the key to Brian's life when he entitled the book *Lead Me to the Rock,* which is a song Brian wrote, the phrases taken verbatim from Psalm 61. It's about a relationship with God, a dependence on God, and a determination to be used by God. Those are the things for which we strive, whether introverted or extroverted.

—Larry Craig, Elder and Church Leader, New York

Introduction

I had a particularly memorable afternoon attending a global discipleship conference in Orlando in the summer of 2022. I was scheduled to speak to a room full of teens and their parents just after lunch, but I needed a few items for an illustration I would give during the lesson. I was scheduled to have lunch with a friend who graciously agreed to jump in an Uber with me to run to a nearby grocery store to get the needed items. After walking back into the arena, I realized I had left my phone in the Uber. My friend offered to go through the headache of getting my phone back from the driver while I hopped on stage to speak. I was stressed by this self-inflicted fiasco, though, and I was trying to switch my brain from the worry of losing my phone and the nightmare that would ensue, to the task at hand. As I stood backstage, I realized that one of my favorite musicians of all time was leading into the lesson. That immediately took my mind off my problems as I locked in to the spirit of worship filling the room.

After the song, I walked out on the stage and could not help but fanboy out just a bit. I didn't plan on it, but before I realized what I was doing, I said to the crowd, "I can't believe I'm up here with Brian Craig. I'm a big fan." It was hokey, but I had never personally met Brian before, and it just came out in a moment of excitement. But in what I would find out was Brian's typical thoughtfulness, humility, and kindness, he yelled back as he walked backstage, "I'm a big Michael Burns fan." To be honest, it was challenging to focus back on my lesson at that point, because the thought that flooded my mind was,

"Brian Craig knows who I am?"

Later that day, we connected, and we stayed in touch from that day forward. The first time we talked on the phone, we started looking for a project we could do together. When I told him that I wanted to write a book on the journey of being an introvert in a church family that has predominantly operated with an extroverted culture, he was immediately all in. To my surprise, we shared striking similarities in our journey. We were both called to public roles in our spiritual walk, something that neither of us would have chosen or ever felt entirely comfortable with. We were both introverts to the core. Brian was not as shy as I am, but he felt like he was a bit shy and could relate to that as well.

We had several wonderful conversations about what this book could look like and what it would be. Brian was excited and told me that even though he had written well over a hundred songs, he had never written a book, and that was something he really wanted to do. Knowing what a gifted songwriter and communicator he was, I was thrilled about the opportunity to work together on this project. Even though Brian had been diagnosed with a type of cancer that affected his brain, he was eager for this undertaking. One time he even told me that he wanted to write a book before he died. I never considered that to be in doubt. It may sound ridiculous, but with every fiber of my being, I believed he would beat his illness and go on to write many books and many more songs.

As we started to explore the specifics of the book, it was more difficult than we at first thought to nail down exactly what we wanted to say and accomplish. We couldn't figure out exactly where we wanted to start and what we wanted to say. Feeling a bit stuck, I proposed that we create a podcast series so we could talk it through in real time and work out our outline as we went. We decided to create "The Misfits" and post the episodes throughout 2024 on the Patreon side of the *Eikon Podcast.* We added a former professional basketball player and devoted follower of Christ, Reggie Hearn, who brought the element of mental health struggles to the series. The plan was to finish the series in September 2024 and then spend the weeks surrounding Christmas to finally complete our book.

I spent the month of October traveling across Africa and putting together our podcast discussions into an outline for the book. It was not until I returned from Africa that I discovered that while I was there, Brian had collapsed and, after a brave fight, went to be with the Lord. I was genuinely stunned. Even though he had been very open about the terminal nature of his prognosis and shared vulnerably on our podcast series, describing how he was processing his ongoing battle, it had never occurred to me that he would not be around to finish this book. In my mind, superheroes don't die. And Brian was a superhero.

I am still struggling with guilt, to be perfectly honest. I feel like most of the delays in us finishing this book were on my end. I did not have the urgency I should have had. I cannot change that now; I simply must learn to live with and accept it. In my mind, the project was dead. We were a team on this. However, as I was praying for Brian's family one morning, I felt a very strong sense that perhaps the project was not done. It was up to me to finish it now.

That is my sole motivation in completing this book. The cover of this book says my name "with" J. Brian Craig. I did not want to list him as a coauthor and give the false impression that Brian was able to put his pen to paper and produce any of the words of this book. Yet not to put his name on the cover would also be misleading because Brian's heart, his thoughts, and his sentiments will be present throughout. Brian's voice, however, will break into the last two chapters especially as I pass on some of his stories and thoughts that he shared on the podcast. There is much more that Brian would have shared that is beyond my ability as a writer to do justice to, and what follows in this book will forever be the worse for that.

I do not want to minimize the role that Reggie played. He too helped to shape the form and ideas in this book. His contributions were invaluable, and that is why his name also appears on the cover as a contributor. Reggie added greatly to the podcast as he described his journey as a professional athlete who struggled with his mental health and eventually found solace in his relationship with God. Reggie's path is worthy of its own book, and I sincerely hope that happens.

Although many of Reggie's church experiences paralleled those of introverts, this book will remain focused on introversion as a case study of sorts. This is not intended to describe the universal experience of all circumstances or cover every category of person who may feel misfit at times. It remains almost exclusively focused on introverts, and specifically shy introverts, and considers how they and the church community can prosper together. My hope is that others who have different obstacles or experiences will find that the suggestions and principles here can apply to their situation, and thus they can prove valuable to more than those who are just like me.

We decided very early on that this would not be a scientific analysis of introversion. Nor would it be an in-depth sociological consideration of the role of introverts in a church context. This will be a personal journey of what it is like to be introverted and shy in a church culture that thrives on excitement, being out of yourself, and all the types of things that are extremely uncomfortable for most introverts. It is about how introverts can find their way and realize that they are exactly how God designed them to be. It documents the spiritual journey from thinking something was wrong with me, to celebrating and appreciating the gift of being an introvert. At no time, however, is this intended to paint the church in a negative light or criticize it. There will be times when suggestions are made that will allow churches to better welcome, embrace, and include those who are shy or introverted or who wrestle with other aspects of their design that can leave them feeling a bit misfit. But that is all done in a spirit of love and appreciation for the body of Christ. I believe that great strides have already been made in my family of the churches to grow in our understanding and inclusion of those who lie outside the lines of what used to be the accepted norm. Introverts, for example, have begun to be honored and given more opportunities to lead and serve. Introverts like Brian Craig have left their unique imprint in churches around the globe and will continue to do so more and more. But that does not mean that there is still not much progress that can and should be made. That is the heart of this book.

There is one other aspect of the book that I will explain before we begin. If any readers have managed to make it through any of my previous books, they will note that I am most comfortable as a writer interacting with Scripture. Those books are full of analysis, exegesis, and application of Scripture. This book will be a departure from that. That does not mean that this book is not scriptural in its inspiration. I would make the case that what follows is a practical application of 1 Corinthians 9:19–23. Paul challenges the Corinthian congregation to embody the gospel that Jesus is the King who draws all nations to himself. This demands that the church be diverse ethnically, culturally, and in every other way imaginable. He calls for a people who strive to be all things to all people. In other words, to be a church that is willing to learn the needs of others and adapt to them as much as possible. Paul concedes that this is grueling but necessary and ultimately rewarding work (1 Corinthians 9:24–27). What does it look like for a church to be all things to the introverted and shy? I'm glad you asked.

• Chapter One •

Different

I don't remember exactly how old I was, perhaps around seven or eight, but I have a clear memory of my parents signing me up for swimming lessons at the local high school one summer. The plan was that my mom would drop me off, I would walk in for the lessons, which lasted about an hour, and then I would walk back out, where she would be waiting to pick me up and take me home to enjoy the rest of my day without school. It all seemed pretty straightforward, or so it would seem.

What they didn't know was that I hated going in there. I was intimidated by the other kids and adults, none of whom I knew. I didn't like to be surrounded by all the activity and noise that echoed through the indoor swimming pool area. And I hated being surrounded by strangers. In short, I did not want to go. So, many times, I would dawdle between the drop-off point and the big glass doors that led into the building. It seemed like the innocent stroll of a carefree kid enjoying every moment of his summer vacation. The reality was far more nefarious. I was waiting for my mom to drive off. Once she was out of sight, I would go back down the sidewalk to an area of concrete around the corner that was mostly out of sight of the drop-off spot and the doors. I would lay my towel on the cement and lounge in the sun for the next hour. Then I would be waiting at the end of the sidewalk with my towel wrapped around my waist, concealing the fact that my suit was not wet, and go home to a day of playing in our yard by myself. A day of playing alone seemed like pure bliss.

I have a thousand stories like that from my childhood. I had friends. I played with and spent time with others. But if given a choice, ninety-nine times out of a hundred, I would have opted for a day alone in my room setting up intricate battle scenes with my set of WWII army men and listening to Johnny Cash albums on my record player. I don't care if you're laughing at me right now. I loved my army men and Johnny Cash back then, and I still do today.

As I moved into high school, I had the growing realization that I was different from many of my classmates. I ate lunch with friends and hung out with them on the weekend, but most of the time I would have preferred to spend time alone. I resisted talking to people I didn't know. I lacked the confidence to speak up in large groups or in class. I kept to myself when possible. I preferred to be by myself most of the time. I wasn't a nerd that couldn't make friends. I wasn't a loner by any stretch of the imagination. But I certainly did not do the things necessary to craft the image of a popular person in my high school. I had no interest in inhabiting such a role.

I may have admitted at the time that I was shy, but that was as far as I could articulate it. Carl Jung introduced the concepts of "introverts" and "extroverts" in the 1920s, but I don't recall hearing those terms in the popular lexicon until well into my twenties. The moment I heard them, however, there was no ongoing mystery. I was an introvert, and I knew it.

Not One and the Same

This book is not a deep dive into the science of introversion and extroversion, but we need to clarify the ideas so that we are all on the same page. I was, and continue to be, both an introvert and shy by nature. Those two often go together, but not always. They are not interchangeable terms. Not all introverts are shy, and not all shy people are introverts. The stories and ideas that follow are from the perspective of someone who is both, so you will have to find for yourself where you can identify with my experiences and where you differ.

What is an introvert? The difference between introverts and extroverts tends to come down to how we process things mentally. It would be a mistake to think that there are two distinct camps with every human being falling clearly into one or the other. There is more of a spectrum, with some people operating on one end more distinctly, some finding themselves more clearly at the other extreme, and other people landing anywhere in between. Some people even identify as ambiverts, meaning they equally display characteristics of both introverts and extroverts.

But let's talk about the classic introvert and extrovert, and you can discover whether you are more on one extreme than the other or somewhere in the middle. For most people, it's not challenging to identify themselves clearly as being one or the other. Introverts live in their own heads. They process information internally, they think before they speak, and they generally find their own thought life more interesting, engaging, and engrossing than external stimuli. Because of that, they seek less stimulation from external sources and can easily be overwhelmed by too much stimulation, whether it be noise, activity, or social interaction. Introverts prefer one-on-one interactions with people they know, not only because of the external stimulation issue but also because introverts hate small talk and avoid it like the plague. It is deeply uncomfortable, as it seems trivial and draining. We also have social batteries that drain quickly and can only recharge when we are alone. The perception is that introverts are all quiet and withdrawn, and many are, but not all. There are introverts who are more in the middle of the spectrum and are outgoing and extremely sociable but are still drained quickly by external stimulation and can only recharge when alone. Because we tend to be deep thinkers, many introverts find themselves in vocations where they are asked to communicate with others on a large scale, which is terribly uncomfortable because we typically do not like to be the center of attention.

Extroverts are the opposite of all that. They think out loud and are energized by external stimuli. They thrive in teams and crowds. They love human interaction and flourish at it. They find energy from being around other people. They enjoy being the center of attention. You can be shy or generally quiet and be an extroverted person, but that is not nearly as common as the typical outgoing extrovert.

Another important difference is that introverts and extroverts tend to process thoughts differently. Most introverts think through words. We have an inner monologue or narrator who comments on and processes everything in our heads. I had always assumed that this is how every human being operated. But no. Many people think in ideas, visual images, and emotions. It is such a foreign concept that it is difficult for me even to conceptualize or describe how a thought process like that might work. In short, approximately 30 to 40 percent of people hear their ideas and most of the rest of you see them, although there are a few rare souls who do both. The inner-monologue souls tend to be more logical and process their feelings through thought, while the visual thinkers are often more emotionally driven and process by speaking.

The recognition of being introverted or extroverted and the impact that it can have certainly did not begin in 2020 when COVID-19 struck, but that event revealed the stark difference between the two. In April 2020, the world came to a screeching halt. Nearly everyone in the United States went into a lockdown unprecedented in our lifetimes. Within weeks, social media was abuzz with extroverts melting down over the isolation they were suddenly experiencing. They were cut off from their main energy source, human interaction, and they hated it. They despised the online church meetings, they didn't care for working from home, and they could do without online shopping. Introverts, on the other hand, started posting humorous memes about how we had been training for this our entire lives. My favorite post said something to the effect of "So you want me to avoid human contact and stay home...to save the world? I can do that."

Extroverts feel lonely when they are alone. In a plot twist that you may not have seen coming, introverts can feel lonely when they can't have time away from people. When introverts are in situations of constant interaction and stimulation, they start to feel not only drained but also isolated. For extroverts, it's just the opposite. When COVID hit, extroverts suddenly got a taste of the medicine that introverts had been forced to drink for years. The online church service came to feel suffocating. It was difficult, soul sapping, and uncomfortable. Many introverts chuckled internally, recognizing that these were the same feelings they had wrestled with for years going to traditional gatherings. This is not to imply that church gatherings are wrong. Nor should we resign ourselves to splitting up, with online services for introverts and stimulating in-person gatherings for extroverts. But for introverts who had struggled for years adjusting to the cultural norms of extrovert-oriented churches and had been told that they wouldn't have these challenges if they were more spiritual, the squeals of complaint were ironic.

There Are More Than You Think

Extroverts seem to rule and dominate the world. In American culture, they are the presumed norm and ideal for human functioning. All default settings are geared to accommodate them. It only seems fair, however, because there are many more extroverts than introverts. Right? Not so fast. Introverts tend to be quiet and less assertive and are thus more invisible, so there are more of them than you might believe. Experts who study these things estimate that nearly 50 percent of the population is predominantly introverted.

If that is the case, then why do many churches seem to be geared for extroverts? Well, not all are. Many traditions, fellowships, and churches are more naturally amenable to quiet meditation, controlled interaction, and limited external stimulation. That has not been my experience. The families of churches that I call home have always celebrated loud, exciting services. They have built themselves on aggressive public evangelism and on relationships. They have exalted those who are outgoing, exuberant, and socially adept, embracing the tacit idea that these individuals are more spiritual and less selfish. They have attained the ideal of "being out of themselves."

Don't get me wrong, I love my church fellowship. I always have and will continue to. But there can be little debate that it has been a movement that has preferred, celebrated, and given center stage to extroverts. I don't believe there was ever an intentional effort to belittle or marginalize introverts, but it happened all the same. Introverts operating in an extroverted culture can be just as exhausted, confused, and out of sync as in any cross-cultural situation you can imagine.

Even though it is very plausible that nearly half of any church is introverted to one degree or another, we have found ourselves outside the norm and in the nondominant position culturally. This has, in many cases, resulted in misunderstanding us and relativizing us as something less than desirable or as people who are spiritually weak or broken. This book attempts to recognize that God intentionally made half of the church like us. He doesn't make mistakes. It is high time for us to imagine what a church would look like that fully and competently acknowledged and embraced both extroverts and introverts.

But Wait, There's More

Not all introverts are shy, and not all shy people are

introverts. Yet there is such a significant overlap that it is not an overstatement to observe that nearly all shy people are, in fact, introverts, and most introverts are indeed shy. I am both, and since this book is primarily from my perspective, it will be written from the perspective of a shy introvert.

Shyness is also something that exists on a spectrum. It's not as simple as saying someone is either shy or they are not. There are degrees to it. Shyness, also referred to technically as timidity, is having feelings of worry, apprehension, tension, awkwardness, or self-doubt during social encounters with other people, particularly strangers. Being introverted describes someone who processes information internally and recharges internally and in isolation. It does not automatically mean someone is shy. Introversion is a personality trait, while shyness is an emotional state. There is no hard data that identifies the percentage of introverts and extroverts that are shy, but research does suggest that a vast majority of shy people are introverts, likely due to the situations created by our preference for turning inward to process our thoughts and our sensitivity to external stimuli.

I would not classify myself as having an extreme case of shyness, but I am definitely much closer to being shy on the spectrum than I am to being neutral or completely confident and outgoing. Left to my own devices, I rarely start a conversation with someone I do not know. I feel awkward and unsure of what to say, and it takes me so long to think about what would be appropriate that the opportunity to speak to the person has usually passed by the time I feel ready to say anything. I have found that when people don't know someone well enough to know that they are shy, they often identify those people as aloof, disinterested, intimidating, angry, rude, arrogant, or some combination thereof.

A church that is not accommodating to introverts is almost certainly going to be even more rugged terrain for a shy introvert. If this is not recognized and addressed, it can leave a person feeling so uncomfortable that they pull back from a fellowship or simply leave the community.

My friend Brian Craig wrote a beautiful song, *Lead Me to the Rock,* based on Psalm 61 that has always inspired me to strive for Christ rather than being reduced to my limitations. My favorite part of the chorus is "Lead me to the rock that is higher than I. You're my tower against the foe." Sometimes, my foe is a crowded room of strangers. Sometimes it is having the social energy to engage consistently with others. Sometimes it is knowing what to say in the moment because I haven't had time to think and process my thoughts. And sometimes, my biggest foe is me. What follows is my journey as a shy introvert in a church world that did not seem to be built for me. I will share my challenges, victories, and what churches can do to lead the shy, introverted, and any category of misfit to the Rock that is higher than I.

· Chapter Two ·

Overwhelmed

I grew up going to church. But when I first visited the Milwaukee Church of Christ in 1998, I knew I had never been to a church like it. I cannot compare the process of feeling like I fit in there to the church I grew up in because I had known those people my whole life. I spent my childhood in that Wesleyan church in Janesville, Wisconsin. I left in my late teens and never attended as an adult, save for an occasional visit when I returned to my hometown to visit my parents. After that, I visited a few churches, and most of them had official greeters at the door, but beyond that, if you didn't want to talk to other people, it was not difficult to slip in, sit in the back, and slip out without a passing word to anyone else.

The moment I walked into the diverse congregation in the MCoC, I knew I had entered an unfamiliar world. Strangers were introducing themselves nonstop. People I had never seen before were hugging my wife and me. People wanted to know our names and learn about our lives. They were inviting us over for lunch. They wanted to exchange contact information and would actually call. It felt awful. That may not sound terrible to you, but it was overwhelming for me. Don't get me wrong. We felt welcomed. We felt loved. In one sense, I suppose, it was wonderful. But at the same time, I felt like this church was full of the kindest people I had ever met, and I also never wanted to return. It was too much. To be honest, if my wife had not been with me, I might have left ten minutes into my first visit with no plans for a sequel. As difficult as it was for me, we came back, but it didn't get better, it got even worse.

The Dreaded Fellowship Break

Back then the church used to have a fellowship break of five to ten minutes during the service. There were plenty of conversations before and after church, but those could be minimized by late arrivals and hasty departures. The fellowship break was different. There was no escaping the fellowship break. They were uncomfortable the first few months when we were still considered visitors. But at least others came come up to me and engaged. That wasn't so bad.

When we were baptized in January 1999 and committed ourselves to following Jesus, there was now an unbridled expectation that I would interact with others, and even *gasp* initiate with other disciples and meet visitors. This was a bridge too far. I adapt quickly, though, and conveniently developed a pressing need to visit the restroom during every fellowship break. That quickly proved ineffective because people wanted to talk just outside the restroom and even while inside. I still maintain that a restroom should be a no-conversation zone, but that's a rant for a different day. I abandoned my bathroom strategy and soon discovered a foolproof plan. If I walked around craning my neck up and around as if looking for someone specifically, people largely left me alone. I had finally found a way to protect myself from the crushing scourge of the fellowship break.

Now, you might ask yourself, *"What could be wrong with a fellowship break?"* It is a way for people to connect and reconnect. It's a time for visitors to meet people and feel welcomed. Plans can be made. Bible studies are set up. I don't deny any of those positive outcomes and many more. Things like fellowship breaks seem completely benign at worst and a huge plus to the community at best. That is, if you look at it from the extrovert's view of the world. For introverts, there are several problems: It breaks the focus and concentration that some would like to reserve for God, preferring to fellowship with others before or after the service. It brings a potpourri of things that can feel hostile to those on the introverted side of the spectrum, from small-talk conversations to the overstimulation of everyone talking at once. Some introverts simply dislike fellowship breaks. But for some, they are painful obstacles to feeling like a normal part of the community. They unintentionally send a constant signal that we are different and even spiritually broken.

When others realized that I avoided fellowship breaks like the plague, I was never once asked why. I was told that I needed to be friendlier. I was discipled on my lack of love for others. The message that these extroverted forms of fellowship and connection were the only acceptable ways to be a Christian was communicated loud and clear. It's certainly not wrong to call disciples to one-another love, but what often happens is that extroverted forms of social engagement are confused with love, which sets up introverts for nothing but failure.

Under Siege

During free-range times of social interaction like these fellowship breaks, introverts can be seized with anxiety over not knowing what to say or saying the wrong thing. The stimulation of everyone talking at once can be overwhelming. One of the biggest fears I had was that there are usually only a handful of people with whom I immediately felt comfortable breaking into conversations. I would look for those two or three people, but if they were unavailable, I would freeze and want nothing more than to run away. What was certain was that any focus I had on God before those breaks was completely broken.

Small talk is excruciating for many introverts. We prefer deeper thoughts and internal processing, and the superficial nature of small talk demands quick responses and witty remarks that we haven't had time to think about. It's like taking a cake out of the oven way too soon. These surfacy dialogues often require sharing personal information, and we don't tend to like that. There is no depth of thinking or emotion to these interactions, and so they drain us quickly. A deep conversation with a trusted friend drains our social batteries like a phone on airplane mode playing a downloaded audio podcast—very slowly. But small talk drains us like a phone using 5G to stream a movie—quicker than you would think.

I understand that the first reaction of many is to point out that my problem was that I was focused on myself and not on God. I disagree. Would those same people contend that the problem extroverts had adjusting to COVID isolation was self-focus or was sinful? Or was the problem the environment?

Thinking It Through

Introverts struggle with spontaneous interactions, so fellowship breaks can often feel like running the gauntlet. We will reserve the final chapter of this book for thoughts on how we might create an introverted-and-shy-friendly church culture while not making extroverts feel ostracized. But I will say here that simply thinking through events like a fellowship break beforehand can be helpful. Try to think like an introvert if you're not one. Better yet, get some true introverts involved in the planning process and ask them how to build features into times like these that can set introverts up for success.

One option that worked very well for me was an experience I had a few years ago while visiting a church in another state. They had a fellowship break but gave everyone a specific question and encouraged everyone to ask at least two other people during the break. This took away the awkwardness and anxiety of what to say. It created a more intimate interaction. And because people were engaging intimately, the overall volume and stimulation in the room were kept to a minimum. On another occasion, the church simply said they were giving time to hug and greet a few people around you. This allowed time for conversation for those who thrive on that, and it gave permission for those like me to give a quick hug, offer a friendly greeting, and move on with no embarrassment because I couldn't think of something appropriate to say. The biggest win of those experiences was that I could tell that people like me had been considered and valued.

Chapter Three

Right Now?

L ess than a year into my journey as a disciple of Jesus, I ran into another series of logs in my road. The men in our church held monthly prayer meetings. But it didn't stop there. We had weekly midweek gatherings that featured thirty minutes at the end for all the small groups in the church to gather and pray together. There were also meetings of various shapes and sizes, which often seemed to end with everyone going down the line and praying one at a time.

"Michael, you're not going to whine about public prayer and assert that disciples shouldn't pray together, are you?" No. Prayer is good. Praying together is biblical. However, there is not one specific method or form of praying that is prescribed biblically. There are ways that we can approach prayer that are exclusively comfortable for extroverts and there are ways that we can approach prayer that could be much more inclusive for minds of all kinds.

The Challenge of Spontaneity

Shy introverts do not like to be center stage. Not only do we need time to think and prepare for such endeavors, but we also tend to be unceasingly self-critical—examining, rehashing, and judging every conversation and public word we utter. We would much rather blend into the background and be left to observe others, think, and only participate when we have something to say that we have had adequate time to craft. The only thing worse than speaking publicly or being in the spotlight is having to do so without warning or time to prepare. To be put on the spot spontaneously? Well, we would rather be dragged around a gravel parking lot by a horse.

Don't forget that extroverts process and think out loud. They don't mind unplanned interactions and public displays. They thrive on all that. Showing up to a meeting and hearing a quick announcement that we will pray by going around the group or splitting into groups of four to pray together sounds nothing but encouraging, uplifting, and spiritually nourishing to them.

For shy introverts, though, lightning sparks immediately begin to shoot through our bodies. Our faces flash hot, and our brains are immediately flooded with regret for being present and schemes for how to dismiss ourselves from this cocoon of horrors.

Introverts typically think about every word and examine it. Did we say the right thing? Could it have been worded better? But if we haven't had time to think, we may feel that we have nothing to say at all, creating episodes of social awkwardness that we would rather avoid. Prayer times with others are no different and leave us with a serious dilemma. When I am put in a position to pray or speak with no notice, I either spend the entire time that others are praying, thinking through what I should pray or intently listen to what others are praying and then stumble and babble on in my prayer, dying inside for the rest of the day.

The temptation for extroverts is to observe many introverts, including myself, speaking publicly and engaging with others very well and then assume that the above is fantasy or selective situational incompetence. "I just heard you give a three-hour workshop a few weeks ago. How can you now claim that you can't pray in public?" That's a fair question.

Many people hate public speaking. More Americans fear public speaking than death and spiders, according to polls. Repulsion to public speaking, however, is not directly connected to introversion or even shyness. When I preach and teach publicly, that is my safe space. I have had plenty of time to prepare. I usually speak about material that I am excited about, knowledgeable of, and comfortable sharing. There is, undoubtedly, a connection that a speaker has with an audience, but they are at a safe distance. I control the terms of the interaction. This may surprise you, but I prefer speaking to a large crowd than conversing with one or two people I don't know. I feel more comfortable teaching in an arena of 5,000 people than speaking in front of a small group of five people. The keys are the time to prepare and the proximity and intimacy with those I am engaged with.

I have taught large crowds. I have attended church gatherings where I was asked to preach minutes before we were to begin. I'm game for that. I have been called and asked to appear as a guest biblical teacher on a podcast with no time to prepare and no questions given in advance. I am down to do that any time. It may appear spontaneous, but it is not, because I have already studied those areas and thought them through thoroughly. I know what I think and what I would want to say and can call on that at any time. But come to me before a service and ask me to give the welcome or announcements or pray, and I will start sweating. I will be in a panic. It comes down to how we are wired. Preparation time is preferred rather than situations that demand spontaneity.

This means that introverts can sometimes appear very outgoing and socially capable, but be very withdrawn and hesitant in other situations. The subtlety of this escapes most extroverts and results in the message being constantly sent to us that we need to "be out of ourselves." The culture of the church assumes that willingness to be spontaneous, and ease in communication in any situation, equals godly zeal and selflessness. It fails to grasp the complexities of the introvert's brain and tells them that they are selfish and sinful.

Can You Pray Like That?

During a recent teaching trip in southern Africa, my wife and I had the pleasure of spending the afternoon with a lovely couple and their children. I love southern African food, and this lunch was not a disappointment. After we finished eating, our wives excused themselves to drop off one of the couple's children at a sports practice, giving the husband and me some time to kick back and chat.

As our conversation deepened, he began to open up about his spiritual struggles. He spoke of the challenges he felt connecting with God or even feeling like he understood how to have a relationship with him. Even though he had been a Christian for decades, the obstacles to a close bond were mounting, and he was developing a sense of hopelessness.

I knew exactly how he felt because I had been precisely

where he was. I couldn't answer all his concerns, but there was something that I had learned that I thought might help him immensely. It took me years to discover, so I was excited to share it with him, hoping it would expedite his time in this particular wilderness. Just to ensure that we were as similar as I suspected, I asked a few questions, and his answers revealed that he was indeed a fellow introvert.

With that knowledge in hand, I began to share my trek of learning to communicate and build a relationship with God. It didn't take me long as a young disciple to realize that something was wrong. Everyone else seemed to love prayer. They spoke of inspiring quiet times, prayer times that left them feeling as if they were walking in the clouds, and of their ever-increasing love for God. That was all Greek to me. Quiet times were a grind. I loved reading the Bible. I could do that all day. But prayer was a constant source of tension. And because I didn't feel like I was ever talking with God, I didn't feel a true connection. The result was that the idea of loving God felt like an abstract theory with no substance or emotion. I was lost. I understood discipline. I understood loyalty. But love? That was a mystery.

I opened up about this with my spiritual mentor at that time and his response shocked me. "Have you told God about this?" His question took me aback for a moment before I finally mustered a weak response, "I can't tell God that I don't love him and don't like praying." He looked at me like I had four eyes and blurted, "Do you think he doesn't know?" As simplistic as that probably sounds to you, it was a revelation to me. He followed it up with some of the simplest but most helpful advice I have ever received. He told me to be honest and tell God and then ask him for help. So, I did.

My difficulties did not resolve overnight, but they did slowly get better as God allowed me to learn things and try new things. I began to understand that who I am and how I am wired are not only okay, that is exactly how God made me. I eventually realized that the gift of being introverted meant that I process information differently than the extroverts who had taught me to pray. I'm grateful for all of them and the walk with God that each of them has, but most of them did not understand me, so they couldn't help.

I learned that introverts don't do well thinking out loud. We are not wired for spontaneity, especially in dialogues. Conversations can present a challenge. We think slowly and deeply. We think about everything. The most interesting area of our lives is often our own thought life. While that can create difficulties, it is also a tremendous strength and gift if understood and utilized properly. With that self-understanding in tow, I began to approach prayer differently.

As we sat on his back patio, we enjoyed the warm South African spring air, and I explained how I had learned to pray differently than I was taught. Instead of just talking to God and employing prayer acronyms like **A.C.T.S.** (Application, Confession, Thanksgiving, and Supplication), I tried other methods. While those can be helpful for many, these approaches were not ideal for me. They left me feeling like I was talking at God rather than doing something with him. My mind wandered constantly during prayer, and I rarely felt deeply connected to God. My prayers felt shallow and routinized. It left me thinking that I was undisciplined and unspiritual and resulted in deep feelings of guilt and inadequacy surrounding my prayer life.

I now spend a good portion of my prayer time thinking with God, I explained to him. Sure, I still have times when I talk directly to God, and I have times when I try to be still and listen for him to speak. But most of my prayer time is spent thinking with God. I invite him in and then think through biblical passages I'm studying or lessons I'm preparing for. I mentally walk through relationship challenges and conversations that I need to have. I think about how I can better serve those around me. Because I've invited God into the mix, we think through these things together. There's a little back-and-forth where I talk, then listen, but mostly I think and allow him to guide my thoughts. This is where I'm at my best. I have new ideas constantly. I walk away challenged, encouraged, and invigorated. I truly feel a partnership with God in a way that I never did when my prayer times were a monologue. I learned to have a relationship with God according to the way he designed me.

Introverts process while thinking, not speaking. I communicate with God in a way that treats the way I was fearfully and wonderfully made as a feature rather than a bug. It revolutionized my relationship with God. The unending guilt about being bad at prayer and having so much trouble building intimacy with God or walking in his love has abated tremendously. This has been a game changer when I'm alone with God.

As I shared this with my friend, I could see his eyes light up. I always worry about sharing this with people, fearing that they will not comprehend what I am saying. But he got it. I think it opened a door for him to pray and relate to God in a way that not only was new but that also instantly feels right for an introvert.

This encapsulates much of the introvert journey in many churches. Extroverts are not bad-hearted. They don't dislike introverts. They just don't understand us, and because so many ministers are outgoing extroverts, the church's culture tends to teach, celebrate, and reinforce the things that work for and make sense to extroverts. Over time, those methods become synonymous with Christian practice and become the norms that are passed on. Introverts try those methods and often struggle without realizing why or that there are other approaches, leaving them in a state of self-loathing and doubt.

So, how did learning this help me be better prepared for spontaneous public prayers? It hasn't. I still face the same dilemmas there. Working on those areas, however, is a lot easier when you have learned to connect with God in a way that honors how he designed you. It helps me to know that rather than something being wrong with me, there are areas in which I can continue to grow, and there are aspects of our church culture that need to expand to become all things to all people.

Give It Time

When we start to imagine what it could look like to create an atmosphere of success for introverts, I am not suggesting that we should be catered to all the time. We don't want to swing to the other extreme so that everything is comfortable for introverts but now extroverts feel unwelcome or uncared for, or cannot utilize their amazing strengths. What I'm suggesting is that when churches think of meeting times, activities, and events, they think about how these will impact introverts. Will it be challenging for them? Does this set them up for success? Will it make them feel judged or invisible? I'm not asking for the culture to shift to exclusively advantage introverts but for options to be added so that the strengths of everyone can be maximized.

When it comes to events like public prayers or speaking, consider options that would include informing people in advance that there will be a prayer time. Give them time to think about what they might say before the prayer begins. Prayers that go around a group in order can be difficult for those who struggle. Consider communicating that publicly praying is an option, but it is also perfectly acceptable to pray privately or to just sit in agreement with those vocalizing their prayers.

Another option to set introverts up for success is to normalize written prayers as an option. Christians have used written prayers for centuries. There are written liturgy prayers over a thousand years old. It's a fairly recent trend in Christianity to view spontaneous prayers as preferable and more authentic. Written prayers give introverts time to think and make the most of their ability to convey deeper aspects of prayer. Think of how incredible a prayer time could be if the spontaneous and passionate prayers of extroverts were offered up intermixed with the deep and contemplative written prayers of a few introverts. Would the church be better or worse? I think the answer is obvious.

Chapter Four

What's Wrong?

I n 2022 I had the pleasure of attending a World Discipleship Summit in Orlando, Florida. If there was an official attendance account for that event, I am unaware of it, but I have heard that, all told, there were somewhere between 15,000 and 20,000 people over the course of the weeklong event. Events like these are brimming with excitement from opening to closing. Everywhere you turn, there are like-minded people who are there to glorify the Lord and fellowship with one another. The music is loud, the lines are long, the rooms are full, and there are crowds absolutely everywhere.

Just walking around at events like this is amazing and encouraging. Okay, let me be honest. It was fantastic for about a day. Then it became too much for this shy introvert. I started to skip out on the music at the beginning of each session and hang around the book tables, which were mercifully quiet and peaceful during those times. During that first day or two, when I was running on adrenalin, I could feel my social battery draining by the minute. I had attended large events like this, but this one was different. At previous conferences, most people didn't know me, and I could walk around as just another face in the crowd. I love that. But at this conference, it seemed that everywhere I turned, someone wanted to talk to me about one of the books I've written or about the *Eikon Podcast*. Don't get me wrong, everyone was kind and encouraging. Every conversation was with someone wanting to thank me or connect personally and positively. But I could not walk down a hallway without being recognized and stopped repeatedly. It was conversation after conversation after conversation.

To make matters worse, my wife had to leave town after the third day, so I was alone in every interaction. It got to the point where I simply could not recharge enough to make it tolerable. I did not have enough time in my hotel room alone. It would have taken me a week to recharge from that much social stimulation. For the last two or three days, I wore hooded sweatshirts in the nearly 100-degree Florida weather so that when I was inside by the crowds, I could pull the hood up, put my head down, walk fast, and hope to get to where I was going without someone wanting to talk. Unfortunately, it didn't really work.

I don't want to give the impression that I am ungrateful for the support. I genuinely appreciate every conversation I had and am thankful for every person who came up to me. I wish that I could process that much interaction better, but I was overwhelmed. And it only got worse with each passing day. It is only now, looking back, that I can enjoy the conference as a memory.

Fellowship Events

Introverts both process and recharge internally. If we are doing anything that involves being around other people in social situations, our social battery is draining. Our battery empties quicker in some situations than in others. Some people drain our social battery faster than others. But make no mistake, if we are interacting with others, the battery is draining.

One New Year's Eve party serves as a perfect example of this. My wife and I had helped plan a party for the singles and campus ministries in our church to help usher in the new year. We had planned for about eighty people, but more than a hundred showed up. My wife did the heavy lifting for the planning and execution of the soiree. She had a food buffet prepared that was so memorable that partygoers still bring it up to this day. In addition to the food area, there were two separate areas to sit and talk or play games, a dance area, and an area to stand and mingle. Wherever you went, though, the pounding beat of the music was ever-present; and partiers populated every available area.

The party was organized so that from the time we began around 6 PM, each hour would focus on a decade. The music would reflect the decade of the hour. Most of the guests had chosen to wear clothes representative of the decade of their choice and enjoyed the ever-changing menu as my wife and others brought out new food options every hour on the hour.

I was amped up for this party and ready to have a good evening. I knew almost everyone there, so I would not have to navigate the awkwardness of meeting new people. Plus, I had determined the playlist, which guaranteed that I liked almost every song we played, so I danced as much as I could. As the evening began, I tried to simultaneously set the tone for the party and play host as I transitioned between dancing with the young folks to get the energy going and walking around greeting everyone. That was the first hour.

As we rolled into the second hour, I may have danced once or twice when a favorite song came on but spent most of the time playing games at the game tables. However, that was secondary to the laughter and fun conversations in the table area.

By hour three, I no longer wanted to dance and didn't have much desire to play games. So I vacillated between mostly sitting and watching others play and finding little duties at the food buffet that needed to be done. The appeal of those tasks was that they allowed me to occasionally exit the party and get out of the music and noise.

With the clock slowly ticking toward 10 PM, I was cooked. I was out of words and out of energy. When an introvert is out of words, it doesn't mean they're angry. It doesn't necessarily mean they don't want to be around others. It's just that the system responsible for thinking of things to say is offline. We are content to observe conversations and occasionally laugh, but that's the extent of it. For the next couple of hours, I sat in a corner a few feet from the game tables. I was close enough to still be considered present but far enough away to easily go unnoticed by those actively playing and talking. But about every ten minutes someone would look over or walk by and ask me, "What's wrong?" or "Are you okay?" or even "Are you upset about something?" They were simply interpreting my behavior by what it would mean if they were doing that, because most extroverts are befuddled by introverts' behavior.

Midnight struck, and before the last lines of "Auld Lang Syne" had reverberated through the room, I was starting to pack up the dishes and supplies and load our vehicle. I had a blast that night but could not wait to go home. This last part might surprise you, but I didn't go to sleep immediately when I got home. I lay beside my slumbering wife and quietly scrolled on my phone for nearly an hour. Why? Because I needed the mental relief of quiet time to myself without stimulation that even sleep cannot provide. Going to sleep will not help an introvert recharge fully. We need time to think and reflect in solitude to truly refill our social battery and energy level.

Over and Over Again

The above story is just one example of what I have experienced countless times. As our social battery drains from interactions and external stimulation, we get quieter and less energetic. We run out of words and are prone to go into energy conservation mode until we can recharge once again. This may take a full day after some events.

Whether at church services, fellowship gatherings, leadership meetings, or small group get-togethers, when we are overstimulated, drained socially, or out of words, it is not something we can just easily change. Yet it is often at those moments, when we are least equipped to explain ourselves, that the questions begin to pour in: "Why are you so quiet?" "Are you upset?" "What's the matter?"

Not all introverts fully understand the phenomenon of being drained socially, so they can't articulate it. Those who are aware don't usually have the energy or desire to explain it. So, we just say, "No, nothing is wrong." That rarely works. Either the questions continue throughout the evening, or the inquisitors walk away thinking that we are rude, selfish, inept, or angry about something. It is rare to interact with someone who recognizes and understands that nothing is wrong, we are just out of juice, and who then communicates to us that it is okay to be who we are.

Where this can become difficult not only for an individual introvert but develop into a problem for an entire spiritual community is when these impressions of introverts are cemented into the culture of the group. Introvert characteristics like quietness, careful listening, and a huge energy capacity for analysis, deep thinking, reading, and studying can be marginalized when positions of leadership or influence need to be filled. Instead, qualities like a sustained social battery, proficiency at small talk, social charisma, and the ability to think and respond quickly are lionized. These extrovert qualities are wonderful, but a community is robbed of all the gifts that God has in store when they are prioritized or emphasized unevenly. It leaves a community with a spiritual culture where introverts never fit the mold for a leader or minister and find it difficult to be considered for such positions. They can and do break through the mold occasionally and often have great impact, but how many were never considered because of the assumption that the typical extrovert qualities are more suitable to ministry and leadership roles? When an introvert does break through and finds themself in an influential role in the church, they are often expected to act like an extrovert. Their ability to maintain that position often depends on it.

One area of ministry that has presented a unique challenge for my depleted social battery is the sermon. Sermons are comfortable ground for most introverts because we have time to prepare our thoughts and control the amount of interaction with others. Even a shy person like me can become quite secure in that environment. Understandably, after a sermon there are often many people who want to talk to the preacher. They want to offer encouragement, ask a question, share an insight, or bounce around some of their ideas. None of that is bad. But no matter how enjoyable the process of preaching is, it is still draining. The result is that the very moment when I am drained and in need of some isolated recharging is the exact time that a line of people wants my attention. It inevitably becomes a massive undertaking of self-denial because I am out of words and social energy and want nothing more than to get somewhere I can be alone. This is one of those areas where there is probably not a solution for this introvert other than some good old-fashioned self-denial. But it would be wonderful if people might recognize the challenge of that and, if possible, save the conversation for another time.

Capacity Limit

The social-capacity challenges go beyond individual events and interactions. These same tendencies in our makeup and wiring can also affect our friendships. It's not that introverts cannot develop or maintain friendships or that extroverts make for better friends. It comes down to an issue of capacity.

Introverts are great friends. They don't tend to dominate conversations. They listen well. All the strengths introverts possess can manifest themselves in making and keeping strong friendships. I have been fortunate to develop some amazing friendships over the years. Introverts tend to be extremely loyal friends, but we do not have the same ability as most extroverts to have many friendships. If we look at my limitations as an example, I have a finite capacity for how many I can give my full energy and attention to at any given time. I can properly maintain three to four deep and strong friendships at most. It is not that I dislike people or do not wish to have more friendships. It comes down to my social battery and my ability to juggle a high volume of social connections. If I try to have more, I will burn out quickly and wind up neglecting all my friendships.

This can be a direct challenge for an introvert involved deeply in a spiritual community. And the problem only worsens for those who wish to enter full-time ministry or leadership roles. We can connect with others, love, serve, and help as many people as needed as long as we properly care for our social battery and recharge as necessary for interactions. However, we will have to be open and vulnerable about our capacity for deep friendships. Without this understanding, we can seem aloof, disinterested, playing favorites, or mean.

The reality is that this often makes introverts more suited for ministry roles like teachers and educators than evangelists and pastors, although I never want to limit or pigeonhole anyone. There are ministry roles that demand high human interaction and an equally high capacity for multiple friendships. I, for one, am not the ideal candidate for those types of positions. I led a church for five years in Wisconsin. The people there were wonderful and kind and patient. For five years I pretended to be an extrovert to the best of my ability. Ninety percent of my job involved human interaction. And I was miserable and consistently felt worn out. When we moved to Minnesota and I took on the role of teaching minister, the majority of my time and role was individually isolated activities like reading and preparing teaching materials. I thrived and was better able to invest in a few quality relationships. Introverts can excel in ministry and leadership roles, yet they do have to be honest with themselves about what facets of the ministry they can best fulfill, given their design and wiring.

Creating Space

One of the biggest challenges of creating a biblical church is to be a gathering of all types of people. That is quite the point of the new creation (Revelation 5:9). The church should be a place of welcome, equality, and inclusion for people of every race, nation, place, socioeconomic status, and neurological makeup. It would be easier to create homogenous church communities. Extroverts and introverts have such different preferences and comfort zones that there is little question that the easiest route for building a church is to either cater to one group's proclivities or to have separate communities. I have personally experienced the former for much of my Christian life. And while I'm not aware of any spiritual communities that are intentionally designed for one end of the introvert-extrovert spectrum to the inclusion of the other, many churches functionally operate that way.

Is it possible to construct a church community that allows both outgoing extroverts and shy introverts to flourish? I believe that it is. What are some areas that can be addressed when it comes to social battery and social comfort zones to accomplish that? Let's consider a few simple ideas that can foster a healthier environment for both.

The first element is to understand the needs of those who tend to be more marginalized in our spiritual community. In my fellowship family, that is typically the introverts. This may seem so simple that it is unimportant, but it is indispensable. Ask introverts what their experience is. Learn about the challenges they have adjusting and fitting in. Determine which of your practices are biblical necessities and which are culturally conditioned. It is also vital for leadership to be familiar with the design and needs of extroverts and introverts and to think through the practices and culture of the church to determine whether there is an imbalance.

The next element revolves around educating the church well. When we consider the needs of introverts in the fellowship and their unique social batteries, it is important to create an ethos that honors the introvert's need for downtime, quiet recharging, and the ability to escape overstimulation without this being seen as a negative action. The church needs to be taught that some people will be out of words or lose steam as a get-together progresses and trained to recognize that this doesn't necessarily signal that something is wrong or that the person needs to be confronted. This will require discernment, but ignorance of this phenomenon and consistently misjudging the situation to the detriment of introverts is unacceptable for a mature spiritual fellowship.

The final element involves wisely planning and constructing events. Has each gathering been thought through with the needs of extroverts and introverts in mind? Not every activity will be comfortable for all, but it cannot be that all activities slant toward one group while neglecting the other. Create quiet spaces that people can retreat to while participating in the event. Build moments of quiet and reflection into a service so introverts can process and have time without overstimulation. Think about options that can be offered in some elements of the service, gathering, party, etc., that will utilize the gifts of introverts and not overwhelm the shy.

The Two Cities Church in Minneapolis-St. Paul had several members who loved Sunday morning church gatherings but had challenges that could make those events difficult. Some were on the autistic spectrum, others had sensory or olfactory limitations, while still others wrestled with social anxiety. They were encouraged, without judgment, to fellowship with the congregation before and after the service as best they could. During the service, a special room was provided upstairs with a live video feed. The group that utilized that room was small. Perfumes and similar odors were prohibited, and the volume could be maintained at lower levels. This room was not specifically designed for introverts, though they were welcome. It served as a shining example of a church that had thought through the needs of all its members and created a welcoming and accepting space for them.

Chapter Five

Am I Broken?

The summer before my senior year of college, I began working for a marketing company that sold high-end kitchen knives. It cost nearly $1,000 at the time for a complete set of them, so they were not cheap by any stretch of the imagination. Making them even more exclusive is that they are not sold in stores. The company operates on a model of sales associates who come to your home, demonstrate the superiority of their products, attempt to sell you knives that you didn't know you needed, and then collect the contact information of your family and friends so they can cold-contact them and start the whole process again.

I sailed through the training and knew the demonstrations and sales pitch like the back of my hand. For the first month, I breezed through one appointment after another with my family and close family friends. They were all kind and generous, and I set a record in the company for most sales in the first month. The sky was the limit, and there was already talk of me becoming a regional manager of an office branch sooner rather than later. But after the first month, reality hit, and my burgeoning career came to a grinding halt. Once I had circulated through people that I knew well, the time came for me to go through the contact lists that each family member or friend had given. I would have to start calling people I didn't know, set up appointments, and convince them to pay a lot of money for knives that they probably didn't need. I spent several days trying to psych myself up to call strangers, but I lost battle after battle with my own courage. Overnight, I went from record-setting sales numbers to goose eggs. I could not talk to people I didn't know. I vowed that I would never again put myself in a position where I had to do that on a regular basis.

And I kept that promise to myself. That is, until my wife and I began attending the Milwaukee Church of Christ. We were asked to study the Bible and found ourselves in a whirlwind of biblical teaching and the calling of following Jesus as a disciple. A big part of that, we were told, was evangelism. It didn't take long to realize what this would demand of me. I was going to have to talk to people that I did not know. Cold contact. Small talk. Constant human interaction. This was not how I had seen my life going. I was going to have to engage in all these nauseating behaviors for the rest of my life.

Going to the Mall

My childhood church was evangelistically active, but as best I can recall, evangelism was almost exclusively defined and practiced as going in groups once a month, knocking on doors, inviting people to attend the church, and then leaving them with an invitation or a tract that explained salvation. I am grateful in many ways to have grown up in that environment, which introduced me to Jesus. But I never developed a faith of my own. At best, I grew up with a borrowed faith, so I felt no pressure to engage personally in evangelism. Plus, I was a kid, so I walked around with the adults often, but never had to open my mouth.

Now that I was an adult who had chosen discipleship with Jesus, I was immersed in a church culture that held evangelism as the centerpiece of discipleship. It was encouraged. It was expected. It was the clearest evidence that you were following Jesus. There are many ways to think about, describe, and practice evangelism. But my new fellowship was an extrovert's paradise. Evangelism could happen anytime, anywhere, in almost any scenario imaginable. But the quintessential picture involved going to a public place like a shopping mall or a coffee shop, striding up to a stranger, and striking up a conversation that would end in an invitation to study the Bible or attend church.

It was terrifying at first. This was not how I wanted to go through life. I had planned to craft my world in such a way as to minimize human contact, especially with strangers. But now it was the substance of my devotion to Jesus. Dare I say that these efforts were considered necessary in that faith community to demonstrate my salvation? This is just how it was. Or so I thought.

What I did not understand at the time was that evangelism was defined and practiced in that spiritual community in strictly extrovert-friendly terms. There was no intent to exclude or marginalize introverts, but it happened, nonetheless. Evangelism became a constant sore spot for me. At first, it felt like a great spiritual challenge I would overcome as I matured. As time went on, it became clear that it would never be easy. Before long, any mention of the topic immediately caused me to feel guilty, inadequate, and ineffective.

I watched others triumphantly share their faith everywhere they went, seemingly with ease. They would get excited about going to a shopping center or spending an afternoon on a college campus. They would return with good news and inspiring stories of people who were open to the gospel message. That's not how it worked for me. The thought of evangelism made me feel sick to my stomach. When I tried, it was forced and awkward. I rarely had any success.

It makes sense. This type of cold-contact evangelism is terrifyingly difficult for people who tend to be cerebral, bookish, shy, sensitive, thoughtful, introspective, inner-directed, risk-averse, and solitude-seeking. None of those characteristics would indicate someone who could excel at extrovert-shaped evangelism.

Is Something Wrong with Me?

It left me feeling like I was irretrievably broken spiritually. I felt helpless because I kept trying but it never got easier. The more I tried, the more I hated it. I never had that breakthrough of success. It became an act of loyalty to God and nothing more. But it was also a constant reminder that there was something wrong with me. I just was not as godly as those who thrived evangelistically.

I questioned whether I truly was fearfully and wonderfully made (Psalm 139:14). As the years passed, I began to wonder if maybe the problem was the emphasis on evangelism rather than me. There is some truth to that, but I was overreacting out of frustration. Sharing my faith with others is biblical. That was not the problem. The problem was that a presumption had been made that certain outreach methods were the spiritually preferable ones.

The reality is that each of us is crafted exactly as God designed us. Introverts do have certain limitations, and with the Spirit's help, we can learn to push past some of them. But when extrovert strategies for evangelism are the only approaches that are taught in new disciples' classes, or are the only versions that we ever see modeled, praised, or endorsed, it creates barriers for those who are shy and introverted or designed differently than the dominant extrovert ideal.

I finally realized that I am not broken spiritually. I was untrained. Imagine taking twenty young aspiring baseball players, all of them right-handed except three, and teaching them all to field and bat right-handed. The lefties would forever feel incompetent. Think of the dramatic change if a new coach arrived one day and began to teach those three how to play the game as dominant left-handers—if for the first time, they were trained in how to bat left-handed and given left-handed gloves. It would be revolutionary.

Think of the strengths that shy introverts like me tend to have. We are good listeners and readers, and adept at analyzing details. We can study material in depth like nobody's business. We are good at reflection, introspection, seeing things from new angles, and coming up with innovative ideas and approaches to problems. We analyze the strengths and weaknesses of systems well. We tend to be sensitive in how we approach and interact with others. We are great students and phenomenal teachers in the right circumstances.

What if the church valued those strengths as much as

the outgoing, magnetic charisma of the average extrovert? What if we taught methods of evangelism that played to the strengths of introverts right alongside the traditional methods of engagement?

Use the Right Armor

There is a small but interesting detail in the account of David's famed showdown with Goliath of Gath. In response to Goliath's taunts and threats against Saul and his army, David asks why no one will step up to the plate, trust God, and take on the great giant. Saul is skeptical but eventually reluctantly accepts the idea of this young man fighting the champion warrior of the Philistines. Before sending him out for the fight, Saul insists on draping David in his tunic, armor, and helmet. The armor simply does not fit. But Saul can only envision him doing this the way he would. To his credit, David realizes that this is a disaster waiting to happen and refuses, choosing to enter the fray with no armor and nothing more than a slingshot.

We often expect others to fit a certain mold and act in ways that keep to the norms of the group. But just because those methods work for some does not mean that they are the best choice for all. As part of a community of believers called to be a light to the world, introverts should be just as committed to offering their lives as an invitation to the kingdom of God as any extrovert. But we should not try to wear their armor while doing so.

Before considering specific tips or methods for introverts when engaging in evangelism or other spiritual activities that demand a certain amount of interaction with others, I will suggest four simple principles to help guide us away from ill-fitting armor.

First, don't feel pressured to act like or be an extrovert to share your faith successfully. Pretending to be an extrovert who is not shy occasionally works for me as a strategy. But I can't do it forever. And it does not work in all situations. It is far better to be myself most of the time and be okay with that. Second, don't feel limited to methods inconsistent with how God designed you to thrive. Third, don't forget that you are most effective when you are yourself. Those are all slightly different ways of making a similar point: Lean into your strengths. The fourth principle, however, points in the other direction. Don't let your strengths, such as solitary studying, become an excuse to withdraw completely, to become a recluse, or to make no effort to grow.

PRO TIPS
Study and Learn

One of the strengths of introverts is our ability to analyze deeply and learn. This is not just true of books. Those of us who feel awkward socially can turn to our powers of analysis and observe those adept at social interactions, impromptu conversations, or inviting someone to learn more about Christ. This will never change who we are, but we can learn and add a few tricks to the bag that we can employ in the right situations. I will never be as clever, quick-witted, or flexible as some of my outgoing extroverted friends are in public, but I can study what they do and squirrel away a few stock phrases and behaviors that will come in handy later.

Get a Buddy

This tip could alternately be called "adopt an introvert." Introverts have strengths and weaknesses, but so do extroverts. Rather than taking the things that extroverts excel at and making them the standard behaviors for an acceptable Christian, let's build communities that utilize the strengths of both.

We moved to Texas in 2022, but before that, we lived in Minneapolis for ten years. I had one of the most encouraging spiritual partnerships with my friend Mike while living in the Twin Cities. Mike is the quintessential extrovert. He spent years in corporate America in sales and similar disciplines, and it shows. He can strike up a conversation with anyone about anything, and within minutes they feel like Mike is one of the best friends they ever had. I marvel at his ability to instantly connect with people and have learned a few pointers over the years. Yet there is a stark reality that I could never fully duplicate his gifts. Although we are very different, we became a great team. Whether we were at a sports arena or on a random elevator, Mike would strike up conversations with strangers before I could even think of what to say. But he never left me standing there awkwardly. He would introduce me and subtly invite me into a conversation. He could effortlessly shift a discussion with someone he just met toward spiritual matters in a way that still boggles my mind. But after getting the ball rolling, he would turn it over to me because we were now in my wheelhouse. He was the opener, and I was the closer. We became an effective evangelism duo because we utilized where each of us excelled.

I've had other extroverts adopt me over the years. I have a couple of friends who are always thoughtful about finding me at ministry conferences and walking around with me, starting up conversations, and introducing me to people. The evangelist of the ministry center in my home church is also my workout partner. Pierre is outgoing and friendly and will not only start up conversations and invite me in, but he also intuitively senses when it's a bit much for me and will take over interaction with another gym goer and allow me to quietly slip back into the shadows of the chat. And when needed, he will always step forward and ask someone using a machine we need how many sets they have left because I think he knows that would be excruciating for me.

But the best extrovert partner I have had, without question, is my wife. She starts conversations, carries them when need be, and takes a step back when she can see I've found a comfort zone and can engage without inhibition. She senses when I am out of words for the day and need to just go into quiet mode. She accepts when my social battery has run out and I need to go be alone. It took her some time to figure all that out, but she is now the best adopt-an-introvert buddy I could ever ask for.

Finding a partner that accepts you in all your introverted glory and partners with you can become one of the most productive friendships and spiritual partnerships you could ever imagine.

Set Up for Success

One mistake a church dominated by extrovert norms makes is establishing a culture where everyone must evangelize according to one stylistic and cultural model that is then confused with *the* way to obey the Scriptures. In my experience, this included the expectations that we all share our faith regularly with strangers, that we set up Bible studies with those who were willing, that we focus our attention on meeting and connecting with visitors to Sunday services, and that we do all by constantly "being out of ourselves."

Healthy, mature, and inclusive churches, however, teach many different methods and roles that provide oxygen to the introvert constantly gasping for air in the extrovert's atmosphere. Rather than wallowing in the mediocrity or failure of believing that my introversion is a weakness at best and a sin at worst, I have found several specific avenues for sharing my faith and taking part in the church's call to evangelism, utilizing the strengths of the way God designed me. These methods should be celebrated and seen as just as valuable in the call to evangelize as more traditional boots-on-the-ground endeavors. Additionally, a wise church will recognize that people have strengths and weaknesses, and they will acknowledge that as acceptable. Not everyone will excel equally at meeting new people or getting visitors out. But as Paul says, one plants, and one waters (1 Corinthians 3:6).

The advent of the internet is an introvert's dream. I can create resources through careful study and in my timing that have a potential reach beyond what I could even imagine. I have had several people contact me in the past few years to thank me for being the catalyst for them to visit a church or begin to study the Bible and become a Christian. These are people I've never met but who have found online material I have created. Not everyone has the patience to research, painstakingly create, and post online material that will draw people to Christ. But many introverts do. Is this any less valuable in the process of drawing people to follow Christ?

Finding roles for introverts to contribute to the work of evangelism, training them as young disciples, and maturing them in the faith will not only help them find important roles within the body, but will also be a boon to the church. Baseball teams don't expect every player to perform every aspect of the game equally well. They maximize each player's strengths. They have players who specialize in defense and are not needed to provide as much offense. They have batters who carry the team offensively but don't play defense. They have both starting and relieving pitchers. The more players they have that fulfill these roles well, the better the team usually is. Or think of a hunter-gatherer society where some go out to hunt, others gather plants, and others cook the food. Each has their role. So it is with the body of Christ.

Introverts may not excel at meeting people and setting up Bible studies, but it is a mistake to implicitly send the message that they are lesser Christians or dead weight in the body. They might excel at the study necessary to answer questions people have about Christianity or the Scriptures as they start to study the Bible to become a Christian. I am capable of taking a seeker through a series of Bible studies to help them become a Christian, but I have become much more effective in the role of snowplow. When someone gets stuck with a supposed Bible contradiction or a problematic doctrine, I come into the study and help clear the road.

Not all introverts are the same, but many excel in the areas of writing, creating resources, and listening to others. We tend to be good at analyzing the needs of a group or seeing potential problems with our systems and methods. If we are asked to develop a friendship with someone who has just joined the community, we are great at locking in on that and being their friend (as long as we're not asked to connect with too many people at a time).

The church that helps introverts and minds of all kinds to lean into their strengths while never giving up on growing in areas of weakness will find that they become stronger and better able to utilize the God-given gifts of all members.

Chapter Six

What If Everyone
Were Like You?

ichael Burns, is anything wrong? You haven't said anything during this entire meeting. I was instantly caught off guard without a good response at the ready for this comment that came out of nowhere during our Zoom meeting. We were on a Zoom call for church leaders, evangelists, and a few teachers. We have already covered the reticence that introverts, especially shy introverts, can have during social interactions. When you add in another layer like video calls, it emphasizes the awkwardness that we can feel speaking up. Introverts are notorious for only speaking when we have had time to think and we feel we have something of weight to add to the conversation. Otherwise, we are quite content with sitting and listening quietly.

Near the end of this hour-long meeting, I had yet to speak. I did not feel that I had anything of significance to add. Suddenly one of the organizers of the call lobbed his question about my lack of participation. Your average extrovert might hear that question and interpret it as a goodhearted attempt to include someone who has not had a chance to contribute. I'm certain that was his intent in asking the question. But for a shy introvert, it was simultaneously a dagger in the chest and the brightest of blinding spotlights being fixed on me. But instead of happily finding myself center stage, I was more like a deer caught in the headlights. We don't like being the center of attention. We don't thrive when put on the spot. And we hate being asked to contribute when we haven't offered. If we had something to say, it would have been said. From the perspective of an introvert, the underlying implication of his callout was that it is unacceptable to quietly observe and to participate only when there is something valuable to share.

As much as I wanted to remain backstage, I was now on the main stage with the spotlight blazing. It was a good thing that I was sitting, because my knees went weak, and a sinking feeling emanated through my body. But every now and then a hero comes along, with the strength to carry. My good friend, James, was on that same call. James is a fellow introvert but not as shy as I am and had been part of that group longer than I had. Before I could stammer and stutter out some inadequate response, James spoke up and said, "Michael is fine. Michael will speak when he has something he feels is worth saying. He doesn't make meetings longer than they need to be." It was like being thrown off a building, hurtling toward my impending doom, but at the last second Superman swooped in, caught me, and gently set me down on the ground.

That moment was so important because it set a precedent for that group. It redefined what the default of a good member of the group was. If James had said nothing, the tacit rule that would have been etched into the culture of that group was that it is not okay for someone to sit quietly and listen in a meeting without generating some comments, even if they have nothing of substance to contribute. And the underlying message to introverts would have been that it is not okay to be designed the way you are—you must pretend to be someone else to fit in here.

Who Has Good News?

There are many ways extrovert behaviors are established as the norm for a church. Two of them that I experienced continually in the fellowships of which I was a part through my years as a young disciple were good-news sharing and responses to lessons in small group gatherings, particularly in leadership meetings.

A normal portion of most leadership and staff meetings I have participated in is a time for sharing good news. This arises from a church culture that values numerical growth and sees constant hype and zeal as the sustenance of spirituality. To emphasize those values and to create a constant aura of encouragement and victory, nearly every meeting began with good-news sharing. From one perspective, we always knew this was coming, so the argument could be made that introverts would have time to prepare for this and have something to share. That's a fair point, but sharing good news still proves to be a difficult situation for most introverts. It goes against our nature, which is to deeply ruminate over events, leading to a more nuanced view of the situation. We don't tend to see everything as just good. We also see the challenges and complexities. So, while extroverts are popping out of their seats to share their latest piece of good news about someone they shared their faith with and who is now studying the Bible, or a serendipitous coincidence that they have interpreted as a "miracle," introverts are wrestling internally with every situation that comes to mind. Is that really good news? Does it measure up in tone and importance to what others have shared? Am I sharing this to bring glory to myself? If I share that story, should I share the discouraging part too, or just craft it so that it sounds nothing short of amazing? Our minds continue to be flooded with questions. Before we know it, the meeting has moved on, and it's one more time that we didn't participate in the sharing. Extroverts then often process this as spiritual malaise or selfishness, because that is what would cause them to not shoot their hand up immediately during good-news sharing.

Even more challenging for my introversion was our tradition of responding to lessons. It is very common in our spiritual family, anytime a lesson or sermon is given outside the Sunday service, to have a time of response. We are expected to stand up and share something from the lesson that really convicted, inspired, or encouraged us. By now you should recognize the many obstacles for introverts. It takes me several hours to analyze, parse, ruminate, and reflect on a lesson I just heard. How could I possibly stand up in that moment and give the semblance of a response that might reflect what I got from that experience? I would rather hear the responses of others, a process that will only enhance my own reflection later. Yet, once again, this can often be perceived by extroverts as selfishness or "being into yourself," a cardinal sin in the extrovert-biased culture.

There is a similar dynamic that takes place in small-group Bible studies. Introverts might contribute something if they feel that they have a fully processed thought that will add to the discussion, but they are happy to sit and listen to the extroverts process their thoughts out loud. This can work quite well unless a culture has been created where contributing to the discussion is the demonstration of how spiritual, how unselfish, and how committed to the church you are.

What If Everyone Were Alike?

I simply cannot count how often I have been asked, "What's wrong?" when I was simply listening and processing what I was hearing. I didn't have anything to share, but it was assumed that I didn't want to be giving to others and was refusing to share. I have been rebuked, discipled, and even had my employment threatened for not participating in the manner and frequency that others thought I should. But I have also been part of groups that have understood my introverted design and have allowed me to be who I am; and I have thrived in those environments.

I was in meetings a few years back where I was new to the group. I didn't know many people in the room, which was a larger environment than I was used to. Additionally, many of the elements of the meeting were introvert kryptonite. They had good-news sharing, spontaneous prayer times, responses to lessons, and even a fellowship break. My introvert's mind struggled to not melt down every time this group met. It was overwhelming in nearly every way, so I responded in a way that had been very welcomed in my previous ministry setting. I was quiet. I observed and processed.

It wasn't long before this was perceived as a lack of interest and buy-in on my part. Because that was the interpretation of my somewhat withdrawn and quiet demeanor, I was called on the carpet and rebuked. I was not asked clarifying questions to explain my actions; their interpretation of those actions was presented as fact. It was obvious what was going on and why, at least in their minds. This was so different from the previous accommodating environment that I had been part of, that this all came as a surprise to me.

During the conversation, one statement/question that was leveled at me was, "What if everyone in the church were like you?" Because I'm an introvert, I did not have much of an immediate response. I listened to what they said so that I could process it later. But it echoed in my mind. What if everyone *were* like me? Would that be good for the church? I can answer that definitively: No. It would not be good. I'm not the first introvert to be confronted with an idea or attitude of that nature. It implies that something is wrong with me. It insinuates that the reserved tendency of introverts and the need to speak only when it is necessary and we feel prepared is not fully Christian behavior. After meditating on that thought for some time, something important occurred to me. It is a loaded question. No one could say that it would be a good situation if everyone acted like them. That is why God formed the body to be made up of many parts (1 Cor. 12:12—26). The church is best when it includes and honors minds of all kinds. I am not implying that I bear no fault or that there are no things I need to learn or be challenged on. But the clear message, intended or not, that was sent to my introverted mind was, "God made a mistake in your design. You must pretend to be something other than your God-given makeup to truly belong here."

Are meetings of the body of Christ better when there are outgoing people who love to fellowship, speak up, be at the center of attention, and talk at every opportunity? Without question, yes. But would it be good if everyone were like that? No. Are meetings of the body better off when they include quiet people who listen intently, process carefully, and whose words are kept at a minimum to emphasize their efficacy? I think so. The more we can recognize that and accept one another just as God designed us, giving room for all of us to be the most maximized versions of who we are, the better.

Recognizing Gifts

When I moved to Minneapolis to serve as the teacher in the Two Cities Church, I had one of the most liberating and formational conversations of my life. I had struggled in my previous ministry position with trying to balance the relational demands of leading a church with the isolating nature of the study and writing necessary to being a biblical teacher. It was difficult to do both, and I constantly felt guilty, as though I were robbing both aspects of my role. Steve, the evangelist in Minneapolis, wanted me to come there to focus on just being a biblical teacher. I am eternally grateful for his grace and wisdom. In our first conversation after I arrived, he said something that was profound: "I don't want you to think about coming out of your office until noon each day." He was not being precisely literal, but I understood the message loud and clear. He was acknowledging the need for an introvert to have quiet time alone to work, think, process, and recharge. He knew that a teacher creates material and needs the time in solitude to prepare. And he honored all that by giving nobility to the aspects of my work that had to take place in isolation. A huge burden was lifted. And it did not stop there. A culture had been created in that church that respected introverts and maximized their strengths and gifts without ever marginalizing or demonizing them. It served as a vision for me of what churches can become if they embrace everyone's abilities and design.

Chapter Seven

A Conduit of Grace

I n a 2024 episode of the "Misfits" series on the *Eikon Podcast,* Brian Craig, Reggie Hearn, and I were discussing the responsibilities of those who often feel misfit in spiritual communities, whether they be introverted, shy, depressive, anxious, or have similar challenges. Do they bear the burden of overcoming their limitations and finding a place in the body of Christ? The conversation inevitably turned to tales of incidents in our lives when Brian and I both allowed our egos to blind us to what our true role was.

Brian captivated us with his story of an evangelistic event for young married couples that was entitled A Night to Remember. The evening's purpose was to introduce newlyweds to the gospel of Jesus and the role it could play as the proper foundation of their married lives. He had been asked to lead a band for the night to play music during some of the intermission and mixer times, a task he embraced with enthusiasm. He worked hard to prepare the band, pick the perfect set of love songs, and then play masterfully throughout the evening. The event was so well attended that they had to run out to get more food, which created even more time for the band to play. And play they did. So powerfully did they regale the audience that it interfered with conversations and connections and instigated several requests from attendees to play a bit softer. But Brian had mistakenly believed that the music was central to the event and knew how hard they had prepared, so he sloughed off any such uninformed entreaties. Finally, the evangelist and organizer of the evening stepped on stage and asked Brian if he could reduce the volume a bit. Irritated by the unmitigated gall, Brian decided to signal how offensive and ridiculous this appeal was. He flicked his guitar pick off the stage and retorted, "Well, we could just stop playing." Having an entirely different understanding of what was important at that moment, the evangelist took Brian's words at face value, missing their intent as a protest, breathed a sigh of relief, and said, "That would be fantastic, thanks."

It was not until later that Brian reflected and realized that his ego had rewritten his role and responsibility in his own mind. He was there to serve, not to be a musician. But his focus had drifted from his role as a sacrificing servant to entertainer extraordinaire. Everything became about him, and that distorted what was important.

Brian was not alone in his hubris. I shared a memory from my college years while working at a historical site during the summer. I gave daily tours and had come to fancy myself as not just a tour guide, but *the* tour guide. During a special weekend event, they asked for the male tour guides to empty trash bins from the unusually large crowds on the grounds while the female guides would give shortened tours. Incensed at this slight, I complained openly about not being allowed to shine. When the site manager called me in to offer a slight rebuke for complaining within earshot of visitors, I rebuffed her thoughts and turned my wrath on her. I was not the problem. I was the star. The real problem was that she was not a historian but a business major who neither understood nor appreciated the history of the site at which we worked. I accused her of being more interested in holding snooty events to hobnob with rich supporters than to honor the history surrounding us. Then, with a flourish, I declared, "You, madam, are a history pimp." What happened next is not a plot twist. She fired me. Unceremoniously. My ego had placed me at the center when it never should have.

Looking back, Brian and I could both laugh at our immaturity and self-centeredness. We were not, however, telling these stories just to make ourselves look bad. We were illustrating how easy it is to get the plot twisted and think that we are the central character when that is not the case. The same dynamic can easily take place when we think of the place of introverts and other misfits in the church.

Where It Starts

Brian, Reggie, and I spent ten episodes of the "Misfits" series exploring the challenges of people who are introverted, shy, or facing other difficulties fitting into the norm. We shared our stories, considered ways churches could be more inclusive, and examined what happens when they're not. But we all thought that it was essential to find the balance. We did not want to end that limited series with the impression that introverts were oppressed victims of the big bad church. We did not want to imply to our listeners that introverts should fully lean into their strengths but never think about their shortcomings, limitations, or areas of needed growth. We did not want people to walk away with the idea that if there were challenges, the church was entirely to blame and solely responsible for change. We were determined to end the series with the responsibilities of the introverted and shy.

Brian was adamant that this whole discussion must start with God. The church's purpose is to reflect the image of God and bring him glory. We are not the main characters. If we concluded our series by implying that introverts bear no responsibility for pushing past limits or growth, that would be putting us in the center place of worship rather than God. Brian had experienced being marginalized and discounted due to his introversion. He was told that he could never be a primary song leader in a church and would never be effective in the ministry. He sat quietly in many rooms while the more loquacious extroverts dominated the conversation. He had dealt with and contemplated all that. He never grew embittered or played the blame game.

Thankfully, he never lost sight of the fact that our journey as a spiritual community is always about God and not us. He desired spiritual practices that formed him into the likeness of Christ rather than merely defending his character and limitations. He grounded himself in God's presence and continually asked himself how he could partner with God. What did God want from him? What did God want him to be part of?

There are equally harmful extremes when we consider the role of extroverts in a church that has fostered an extroverted culture as the norm. On one end, we can demonize or marginalize introversion, giving the impression that it is inherently missing the mark of what a Christian should be. This puts the onus of change solely on the introverted and shy. They are the problem. They must grow. They must adapt. They must mature.

The other extreme paints introverts as victims. The church must anticipate and accommodate every need and preference. The shy person must never feel uncomfortable. They must never be challenged. The church is the problem. The church must grow. The church must adapt. The church must mature.

In either extreme, we have erroneously placed humans at the center. When we remember that it starts with God, we will keep in our sight the importance of sacrifice and acting in the interests of others. Paul declared to the Corinthian congregation that he was free, yet he would make himself a slave (1 Cor. 9:19). He would adapt and change and grow. He would do so voluntarily. But he also called every individual within the church, and the church as an organism, to carry the same mantle. When only one portion of the body is being all things to all people (1 Cor. 9:22), imbalances develop. When we are all doing it, something wonderful emerges.

A Living Sacrifice

One of my favorite classic YouTube videos from the early 2000s features the Christian comedy duo Johnny and Chachi singing about the nuances of unity and working together. In their "Teamwork" video, the straight man, Johnny, introduces the song by declaring that teamwork is "less about me, but more about we." The delightfully goofy character, Chachi, responds by saying, "We all know there's no 'I' in team, but there's also no selfish hypocrisy in team either." Truer words were never spoken.

Of course, teams are composed of individuals, but if we give center stage to the individual, the collective quickly disintegrates. Paul captures this succinctly, stating that disciples are to "offer [our] bodies as a living sacrifice" (Romans 12:1). He asserts that this is pleasing to God and the embodiment and substance of Christian worship. Becoming a living sacrifice enables the spiritual community to know and live out God's will. Paul's wording in Romans 12:1 is enlightening. He acknowledges individuals by urging them to offer their "bodies." Yet, it is interesting that he does not say, "Offer your bodies as living sacrifices." Instead, he calls each of them to offer their "bodies" as "*a* living sacrifice." He acknowledges the plurality of their many individual bodies but calls them to become a singular sacrifice together. This is how they worship God. In other words, they are each to die to self to become the collective body of Christ. The many become one. There is, simply put, no room for selfish hypocrisy.

When we start with God, our situations play a role, but never dominate the story. We see the world through a God-focused lens rather than one of self-focus. This brings the necessary balance of being all things to all people. The individual strives to use and maximize their gifts, but it is to serve others and build up the body. Who I am is important, but not to become the star or the center of all attention and resources. I am willing to adapt and grow. I am not alone, however. We should all be actively doing that. And as the church as an organization constantly strives to be all things to all people, it becomes an environment of sacrifice for the benefit of others where we seek to outdo one another in honor, inclusion, and acceptance.

The Flow of God's Grace

The Apostle Peter puts it like this: "Each of you should use whatever gift you have received to serve others, as faithful stewards of God's grace in its various forms" (1 Peter 4:10). Once again, we see that God is at the center. We are stewards. Like Paul, Peter emphasizes that each person plays a part. We have all been given gifts. But the gifts are simply tools, not the main point. Each person should maximize their gifts for the benefit and edification of others.

Paralleling Peter's thoughts, Paul followed his call to be a living sacrifice by summoning the church to "not think of yourself more highly than you ought, but rather think of yourself with sober judgment, in accordance with the faith God has distributed to each of you" (Romans 12:3). Peter and Paul agree that every Christian is unique. We have gifts, talents, abilities, and compositions that make us valuable and useful. But they are in unison in teaching that this is not to exalt or bring glory to us. It is to build up others and to glorify God in the process. Not everyone has the same function, says Paul (Romans 12:4), but we form one body and, thus, belong to one another (Romans 12:5).

Notice that Peter says we should use our gifts to serve others, then he takes it one step further. When we do this, we become the conduits through which God's grace flows. Don't overlook the significance of this. God gives each of us many gifts, and those gifts are the ongoing channels of his grace. If I don't use my gifts or the spiritual community mutes my gifts, God's grace is partially blocked. We are robbed of the full measure of his grace that he wishes to share with us. If I fail to maximize the full potential of my introvert makeup for the glory of God and the service of others, it is my brothers and sisters who are cheated rather than just me. A church that celebrates and makes space for extroverted gifts only, misses out on a significant portion of God's grace. This is important because whatever it is, we can't do it without God, but God won't do it without us.

Each of us must be present, be active, and seek to use the way that God designed us so that God's grace can flow and overflow in the church.

The Pivotal Choice

One of the more popular slogans or mantras in the modern world is some form of "Be true to yourself." We see versions of this everywhere: Have it your way. Look out for number one. I was born this way. You do you. Put yourself first because no one else will. Seek happiness… It is truly ubiquitous. Every single one of those statements preaches the value of putting self on the throne.

Jesus' message was markedly different. Rather than encouraging his followers to be true to self, he called his disciples to die to self. Dying to self, though, does not mean becoming spineless. It does not entail being a doormat. It means that the focus is on God's people and others rather than me. I can honor how God designed me and seek to create space for me and others like me to thrive, but not because we are looking out exclusively for our enrichment. It is to serve others as a vessel of God's grace. When I recognize, honor, and use the gifts God gave me, the body of Christ wins.

But that will mean that not everything is going to be about me and my gifts. My gifts won't always be perfectly used. There is no way a church can allow everyone to use every gift they have at all times. If my mentality is self-focused, I will not be open to compromise. I will nitpick when an activity favors extroverts. I will devolve into seething when my strengths are not highlighted. I will consider leaving the church if I'm not catered to.

Yes, I am an introvert. But that cannot be the end of the story. There needs to be balance. I cannot demand that the church accommodate my every whim, preference, need, and desire. If the church makes an effort to be all things to all people, and I choose to die to self, the beautiful community flourishes.

My Part

I love being an introvert. I'm grateful that God made me this way. There are many positive aspects to the way I am designed. But there are limitations. It will take discernment and being a living sacrifice to know when to assert my strengths and create room for them in the church's culture and when I should be called upon to push my boundaries and grow.

It helps me to be aware that there are four levels of learning and accountability. Some things I do well without effort or accountability. I don't need to create an accountability plan for reading or spending time in deep thought. That will happen automatically. The next level is internal accountability. There are some areas where I need to grow but can do so steadily with a plan that keeps me accountable to myself. For instance, I don't love talking on the phone, but if I create a list of people I should call this week, I will do it. I can help myself grow by holding myself accountable. The level beyond that is external accountability. There are things that I will not do unless I am vulnerable to others and ask for their help. If I want to pray with other people regularly, I will fail with only self-accountability. There are too many obstacles for me to be consistent in that area of my life. So, I must share it with others and ask that they hold my feet to the fire. Finally, there is professional accountability. Some things are so entrenched that I may only be able to grow with professional help or therapy.

When it comes to growth and pushing myself beyond my boundaries and limitations in a church community, there is an important caveat. It is okay for others to suggest areas in which I might need to grow or lovingly challenge a limitation or boundary, but it should be relationally, not culturally. This means that introverts will not ideally be pushed to go beyond their comfort zones through the structure or culture of the group. This is unfeeling and usually unloving. It does not honor the gifts of all members of the body. Will there be norms? Yes. But there should always be consideration given when planning things and, when possible, options should be provided. If there are times when I need to be pushed a little, the most effective means to that end is through a relationship.

For example, let's say that several members of your small group don't like to speak to visitors. They rely on extroverts to do that and simply avoid it at all costs. Don't respond by having discussions built into the lesson where you intentionally pair them up with a visitor. That may work, but it might create resentment and result in them eventually avoiding coming to the small group. It would be far better to respectfully set up time with them and ask them carefully thought-out questions about why it is difficult for them to talk to new people. Together, you can come up with a reasonable plan to help them grow in this area. This will be far more effective than forcing them into it through the structure or cultural pressure in the group.

The best way for introverts to grow is if we see the need and make the effort or ask for help. Keeping in mind that I am part of a living sacrifice, I am determined to be fully who God made me but also adapt where I can and progressively push myself beyond my perceived limitations when possible. It will always demand discernment and balance. Introverts can grow past many of their social obstacles, yet what we cannot change is how we are wired to think, process information, and recharge. There is no need to change those things.

But we will not always see areas where we can grow or should ask for help. If you do think you see a situation where an introvert needs to push past some of their limitations, then keep these principles in mind. Do not publicly shame them or embarrass them for who they are and how they are designed. Do not imply that their introverted tendencies are sinful. Do not be harsh with them. Ensure that you have taken steps to guarantee to the best of your ability that you are not imposing your opinions or preferences on an introvert. Do not make assumptions based on your ignorance of introverts or a bias for extroverted behavior. When you talk to them about ways that they can appropriately act for the benefit of others, it should be done keeping in mind how God designed them and in such a way that sets them up for victory. We are striving for everyone to be mature in Christ with the gifts God gave them, not for every Christian to live up to an extroverted ideal.

During our podcast discussion, Brian pointed out that the balance of introverts growing past boundaries and church cultures changing to welcome, celebrate, teach, and utilize introverted gifts will always be messy. But, as he reminded us that day, God put us together to work it out. That is precisely what it means to be part of the body of Christ.

Chapter Eight

A Church for Everyone

I never planned to go into a full-time ministry vocation. I studied to be a historian and thought that would be my life's path. Then I became a disciple of Jesus, and things began to shift. A few years later my wife floated the idea, and some agreed that it would be a good path for me. Others were skeptical. I didn't fit the mold. I was quiet, introspective, and not a top-notch people person. There was a need, though, so I thought I would do my best to fill it. Just a few weeks into the role, the ministry staff from our local church was going to a meeting that included all ministry staff personnel from all the churches in our movement from the Midwest.

I was terrified as I walked into the first meeting. There were over a hundred people in the room, and I knew just a few people, who quickly scattered throughout the room. This was my worst nightmare. I already felt unworthy of being in the ministry and was intimidated as a young Christian by all these well-known and well-established ministry icons. "Nope, not today," I thought to myself as I gazed across the spate of conversations and started making my way back to the door. I had already formed a plan to go up to my hotel room and stay there alone for the next two days, hoping that no one would notice.

Just then I felt a hand on my shoulder and a friendly, piercing voice boomed, "You're Michael, aren't you?" I turned around to see the beaming smile and warm face of a highly respected elder from Chicago, Jeff Balsom. Jeff has since gone to be with the Lord, but he was sharp and could read people. Even though most ministry people are charismatic, outgoing, and great at building relationships, I think he could sense that I was not that guy. He put his arm around me, got a little closer to my ear, and quietly said, "C'mon, let me introduce you to a few people." For the next ten or fifteen minutes, Jeff walked around with me, starting conversations and letting people know who I was. It was a small act of kindness. I never asked him about it, and he probably would not have even remembered it years later. But for me, it made all the difference in the world. It transitioned that hotel meeting space from a room of horrors to a place for me. He didn't rebuke me for being shy. He didn't challenge me to be more out of myself. He was compassionate and thoughtful. He adapted the environment for me and allowed me to be authentic while giving me the footing to push past some of my boundaries.

Throughout this book I have attempted to share my own experiences along with some suggestions of how introverts and the shy can push past some boundaries they may have as well as how churches can create a welcoming environment for them. In this final chapter, I will propose six principles churches can adopt to help orient them toward being a place for all kinds of people.

When we began our podcast series, "The Misfits," I thought we would breeze through the list of principles I had created in one episode. But it quickly became clear that it needed work. On the fly, during the first episode, we shifted, and together Brian, Reggie, and I reworked these principles throughout the next six episodes. What follows is my best attempt to summarize our work on the podcast to prepare the material we needed for this book.

A Culture of Consideration

Imagine that you work in a large, beautiful public building. Each day you climb the imposing stairs leading up to the front doors. You descend the stairs in the evening, go to your car, and drive home. What you likely never think about is how privileged you are to be able to ascend and descend that staircase each day. Those stairs are not accessible for all. There is no ramp or lift. That may not ever pass through your mind until you see someone in a wheelchair. But they will notice the problem immediately. They will discern the lack of access but also be instantly struck by how little they were considered. It's not that anyone intentionally excluded them. Instead, a signal was sent that they were not worthy of consideration. They do not fit the norm. They are a burden. They are not truly welcome here. This is exactly how shy and introverted people often feel when a church's culture has not considered them as part of the normal human experience.

One of the reasons that we had Reggie join our podcast series was not because we wanted a third introvert in addition to Brian and me. Reggie is not an introvert at all. But he has battled mental health challenges like depression and anxiety, especially when he played in the NBA. We thought that bringing in that element of those who can feel like misfits in other ways would be helpful for the podcast discussion. While I have kept the focus in this book more narrowed, much of what Reggie shared from the perspective of those battling mental health challenges applies to introverts and many other experiences and has helped shape what follows.

Reggie noted that an important part of feeling considered by a community is when it becomes clear that they have taken the time to understand how hard this can be for someone in his position. Whatever our challenge is, we don't want to be alone in it. When we arrive at the bottom of the stairs and find no ramp, we know that we have not even been on your mind. We feel alone and excluded. The word "understand" visualizes you standing under my burden with me. It is true that God is the only one that can perfectly do that. No human, and certainly no church community, can ever do this completely. We cannot have that expectation. But it is important for churches to consider the needs of everyone who is or could become part of the community. Just knowing that the church family has done their best to think through my unique design and create the solid ground on which I can stand and from which I can grow is a game changer.

The best way to create a culture of consideration so that people don't feel that they are little more than a burden to the community is to take them into account. Invite input from different elements of the community. Give them positions of influence and a voice to express their needs. There must always be a balance, and not everyone can or should be catered to all the time. We are creating a community of self-sacrifice. But in doing so, a strong culture of consideration for all will allow all to flourish and thrive.

A Culture of Visibility

A common experience for many introverts in the church is that if they want to be fully accepted or be considered for leadership and ministry positions, they must act like extroverts. I would be the first to admit that a painfully shy person cannot let that trait dictate everything they do and at the same time want to lead and influence others. That would be incredibly difficult, if not impossible. However, introverts and those of us who are shy are often discounted or excluded, not because we are not effective, but because how we interact with others in public or how we lead does not fit the expected extroverted culture. It leaves us feeling that we are invisible in the body. No one sees us or appreciates us for who we are designed to be.

There are many names ascribed to God in the Old Testament that capture various aspects of his nature and character, but none more encouraging than one found in Genesis 16:13 where Hagar calls God by the name El Roi, the God who sees me. Everyone else around Hagar has treated her as disposable, but not God. God sees her for who she is. This is so unusual for her that she recognizes and names it immediately. She has been seen and accepted by God.

When churches make clear that they have considered the needs of more than just the ideal extroverted, charismatic, fired-up, outgoing disciple, they send the unmistakable signal that we have been seen. Without this, it is easy for a group to send the message that the only acceptable state is for you to meet that ideal. Anything outside of that is a drag on the community, or worse, it is a sin unrepented of. That was the implicit message I received many times early in my faith walk. My introversion was not a gift. It was the problem. It was a weakness. I needed to be zealous and exuberant to show that I was faithful.

Imagine a midweek service where it is announced that they are splitting into small groups for ten minutes of prayer but also stated that there is a section of the room for those who wish to pray privately by themselves. Think of reading the church's weekly newsletter where you see an announcement for a new series on how introverts can share their faith and impact those around them. How would the introverts feel? Would they feel seen and embraced by their brothers and sisters in a whole new way? Would they be encouraged? The answers are obvious.

A Culture of Being Heard

One of the quickest ways to foster a feeling of disaffection and not belonging is to allow a group of people to feel they are not being listened to. When the Grecian Jews voiced their concerns of neglect with the leaders of the Jerusalem fellowship, the leaders listened and responded immediately. They were careful not to ignore their concerns. We have no record of the leaders pushing the blame back on the marginalized. Instead, they asked them to choose men from among them who would take on leadership positions for the whole Christian community, both Hebraic and Grecian Jews. Being heard is about representation and having a seat at the table.

It is a good first step for ministry and church leadership teams to assess whether they have included diverse voices. Some churches have made impressive strides to do so racially or with genders, but few have ever considered whether the voices of influence are dominantly or exclusively extroverts. Inclusion of this perspective can become even more difficult when we know that simply having one or two marginally introverted leaders, often the "teacher types," will not always adequately represent the needs of that community. The reason is that introverts who have risen to those levels of influence within the church culture have learned to adapt and have been enculturated over time. That doesn't render their voice meaningless, but it does mean that they may not always fully understand the struggles of those without influence or a voice. Efforts need to be made to hear from those within the present leadership structure as well as from outside the normal avenues.

When introverts are included in positions of influence, are they fully accepted for their strengths and allowed to advocate for others like them? For example, most of the introverts I know in ministry positions in my global fellowship are teachers. And most teachers are introverts. If you don't believe me, go to a conference for church leaders and evangelists and then go to one exclusively for teachers. The differences are striking. Remember, though, that introverts tend to be introspective and carefully analyze everything. This means they will often question the status quo, offer critiques, point out areas of dissonance and things that could be improved, and employ an edge of prophetic imagination. Because most teachers are wired like this, the above sentence fairly describes most of the biblical teachers I have known. Most evangelists are extroverts. This is not to say that they do not think about things or analyze processes. But they are gifted in different ways. They want to energize, move, coalesce, and build. They don't have time for the type of reflection and correction teachers thrive on. This creates tension and often leaves church leaders looking for ways to minimize the role of teachers rather than recognizing the tools they possess as gifts from God and building them into the culture. In some places, this has been done well. But in many others, it has not.

Consider the various subcommunities in your congregation. Are their needs considered, and is their voice properly heard? Does your church listen to introverts and the shy? What about nondominant cultures, those with mental health struggles, the chronically ill, the neurodivergent, etc.?

A Culture of Confidence

Many aspects of being a Christian seem like they are exclusively in the extrovert camp. From the start, the deck feels stacked against introverts. Christianity is about community, fellowship, evangelism, connection, corporate activities, and on the list goes. It is easy to see how we might wonder if introverts can be themselves and truly be Christians. This only happens, however, if we create a caricature of introverts in our minds. We cast introverts as misanthropic hermits who want no part of a community. We start with their weaknesses rather than their strengths. Yet we don't tend to create a similar negative stereotype of extrovert traits. If we did that, we could describe someone who is overly friendly, relationally needy, and shallow, with no ability to study or think deeply. This negative stereotype creates cartoon characteristics that are barely distinguishable from a golden retriever's.

We have already discussed how easy it is for churches to subtly send the message that there are no introvert-based ways to fellowship, evangelize, and be community. The message that we must transform into godly extroverts or continue in sin becomes internalized. Rather than a gift from God, introversion is seen as a weakness from which to be repented.

In 1 Corinthians 12:12–26, Paul trained the Corinthian church in godly diversity. He taught them that they should not mimic the divisive social stratification of the surrounding culture, but instead realize that those of higher nobility and status need those who are lower. God has put them together, Paul argued, so that they would be mature, complete, and a true picture of united humanity. The principles of this teaching apply to the topics of this book. A mature congregation has not simply trained everyone to be out of themselves so that they are proficient at being or pretending to be an extrovert.

A mature fellowship does not leave a significant portion of its people constantly questioning themselves or being questioned. It creates confidence in who God made them to be, while at the same time calling them to continue to grow spiritually. This means that extroverts will grow spiritually but in ways consistent with being an extrovert. And introverts will grow in a manner consistent with their unique design.

Paul taught the Corinthian believers that rather than celebrating those of high social status, they should intentionally nurture and advance those of the lower and weaker status-es. If we follow this principle, then does it not follow that we would resolutely do the same for the misfits among us?

A Culture of Belonging

One of the most powerful elements of a healthy spiritual family is the ability to know others and truly be known and accepted for who we are. Don't confuse this with groups with no transformation or spiritual growth standards. It is a rare place where you can fully be yourself while transforming to become more like Christ uniquely. Too many churches that take spiritual maturity seriously devolve into forming people into a singular culture or model rather than encouraging each person to lean into the strengths of their exceptional design.

As we have seen throughout this book, it can be elusive to create a culture where both extroverts and introverts can mature and develop in their own way without casting one group into a category of judgment or inferiority. In extrovert-biased spaces, it can be challenging, if not impossible, for introverts, the shy, or those who struggle with self-confidence to feel that they can be themselves. This leads to them never finding a place where they are known. And that will eventually wear thin for most people.

Everyone has their own life struggles as well as spiritual challenges. It is not easy, however, to comprehend the challenges of others who are not like us. As a shy introvert, I constantly battle things like imposter syndrome and feeling that I don't fit in anywhere. This can present serious obstacles for me to know and be known, because when people say they are my friends or want to spend time together, I have difficulty believing them. I convince myself that they are merely being nice. I won't call friends because I feel like I'm bothering them. I will avoid making social plans with others because I believe they are only doing so out of obligation, and I would be intruding. Add to this my introverted temptations to not want to talk on the phone, to give in to my low social energy, or to avoid impromptu plans, and those around me can quickly get the feeling that I am aloof, too busy, or don't like them.

During one episode of "The Misfits," Brian shared about two ministry leaders he worked under in the 1990s. The first built a strong relationship with him and made it clear through his acceptance of Brian's introverted idiosyncrasies that he cared and wanted him around. The leader who replaced him demonstrated just the opposite. Brian could sense that his gifts and temperament were not valued. The first leader, said Brian, got on him more and made more mistakes with him, but Brian could operate much better because he knew he was wanted and loved. That's important for introverts because we analyze everything, and if we think people don't like us and don't really want to know us, we will shrink deeper into our comfortable internal world.

A huge part of creating a culture of belonging where we are known lies in self-responsibility. Others will not know the unique obstacles to building a relationship with me unless I am vulnerable. The church will not know how to adapt and educate to foster a welcoming culture if enough of us aren't willing to be open and share our insecurities. Knowing and being known is a two-way street of vulnerability and caring.

Many introverts desire community but lack the tools, the drive, or the courage to make and maintain a role. They will have to be drawn out on occasion. My personal appeal here is to not give up on us. Bear with us in love and make the effort to truly know us, and the church will benefit and grow stronger.

A Culture of Being Wanted

Introverts often become accustomed to the shadows. We learn that we do not match the ideals of our culture. Plus, most of us are uncomfortable with the spotlight, so we won't put up a big fight if we are marginalized or merely tolerated in a culture. I'm unaware of any church that will advertise, "We only want you here if you will repent and act like an extrovert," but that message gets communicated in many ways. Let me be clear, I have seen great progress in my spiritual family. Over the decades, I have seen more introverts in ministry, embraced in the congregation, and thriving as they are allowed to use their gifts. But there is still much work to be done. Many church cultures have not ever been examined and maintain the extroverted bias they have had from the moment they were planted as a congregation. When the normalized practices, teaching methods, and ideal behavior in evangelism, fellowship, group design, meeting culture, worship style, and activities are structured and geared for extroverts, it sends the signal that the rest are being endured but not truly wanted.

Churches will never perfectly include and maximize every type of gift and every member. But that should be the goal, and we can never stop trying. Extroverts and introverts can revere and appreciate one another and strive together to reach "the Rock that is higher than I."

CROSSING THE LINE
CULTURE, RACE, AND KINGDOM

MICHAEL BURNS

Available at www.ipibooks.com

POLITICS, ALLEGIANCE, AND KINGDOM

ESCAPING THE
BEAST

MICHAEL BURNS

Available at www.ipibooks.com

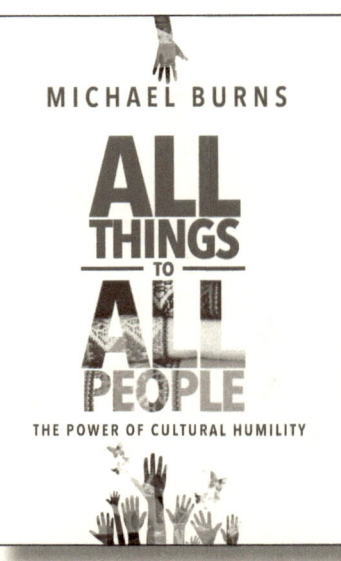

MICHAEL BURNS

ALL THINGS TO ALL PEOPLE

THE POWER OF CULTURAL HUMILITY

MICHAEL BURNS

A CROWN
— THAT —
WILL LAST

A 7-WEEK DEVOTIONAL
ON CULTURAL HUMILITY

Available at www.ipibooks.com

Available at www.ipibooks.com

Welcome to the New

ILLUMINATION PUBLISHERS
www.ipibooks.com

SPEAKING OF GOD — DR. JOHN M. OAKES

Spiritual Transformation — Cresenda Jones

MESSIANIC JUDAISM — DOUGLAS JACOBY

Go in the Strength You Have — Rayola Osanya

A HOUSE OF PRAYER — C. SCOTT DAVIS

LOVE, LAUGHTER, AND LAW — RON AND LINDA BRUMLEY

Jesus and Mental Health — Marvin K. Lucas

WHAT NOW, GOD? — JEANIE SHAW

SINGLES MINISTRY CAN CHANGE THE WORLD — FERNANDO ALEJANDRO

Mindpowered Singles — CRESENDA JONES

Journey of the SOUL — Timothy Sumerlin, Editor

THE UPWARD CALL — PAT GEMPEL, EDITOR

CALLING OUT THE PEOPLE OF GOD — DOUGLAS JACOBY

PAIN KILLER — R.K. McKEAN

The Sacred Journey — Jeanie Shaw and Friends

WILDFIRE — DAREN OVERSTREET

The Recovery Journey

This Doesn't Feel Like Love Either — TIMOTHY SUMERLIN, Ph.D.

LAMBS

www.ipibooks.com